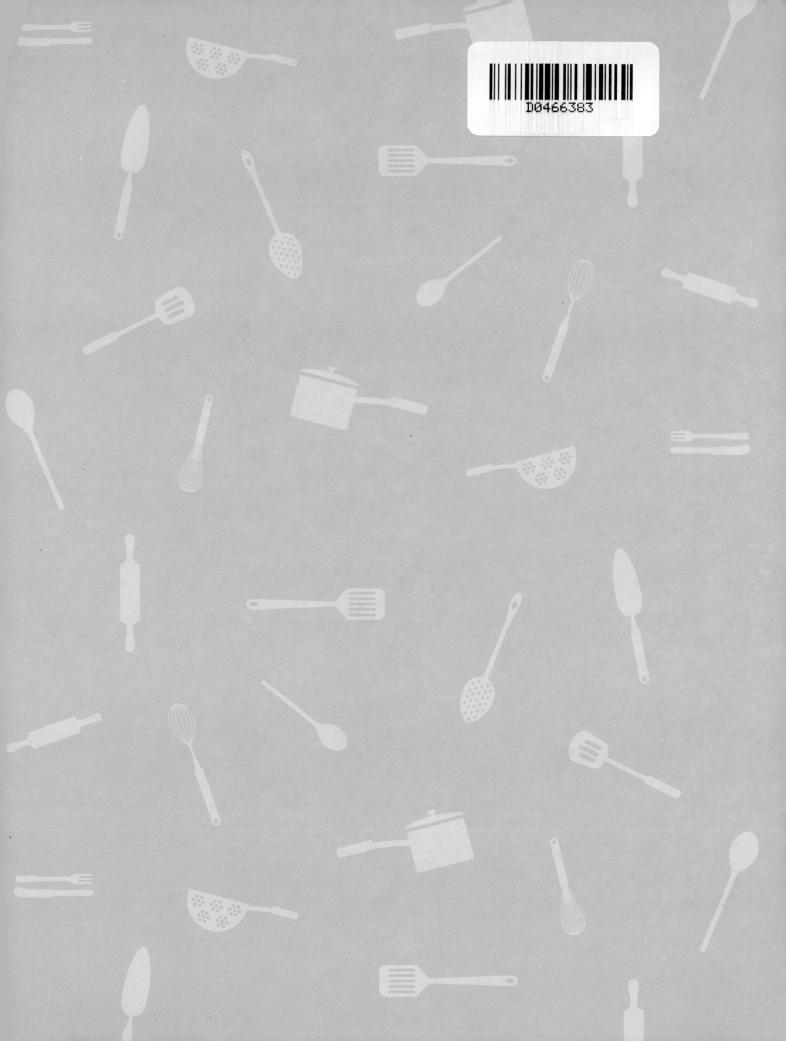

MAKE, BAKE AND DECORATE

CUPCAKES

BY NANCY LAMBERT

PUBLISHING PLC

Published by Top That! Publishing plc
Tide Mill Way, Woodbridge, Suffolk, IP12 IAP, UK
www.topthatpublishing.com
Copyright © 2010 Top That! Publishing plc

CONTENTS

INTRODUCTION

The term "cupcake" was first used in an 1828 cookbook and got its name from the individual pottery cups they were baked in. Since then, the little cakes have enjoyed much-deserved success and have grown even more popular in recent years. From the mouth-watering frosting to the fluffy base, a fantastically made cupcake is guaranteed to appeal and bring a smile to anyone's face!

This book will provide you with a selection of cupcake recipes that are perfect for junior chefs to make with the help of an adult. And remember, once you have perfected the recipes, don't be afraid to experiment with the ingredients and toppings to create your own great cupcake treats!

COOKING TIPS!

- Make sure you use the freshest ingredients possible.

- All of the cupcakes in this book feature butter, but margarine spread works just as well.

- Fill your cupcake cases so they are about two-thirds full. Don't fill them too high or they will spill over whilst in the oven.

- Cupcakes are best eaten the day they are made, however plain cupcakes can be frozen for up to three months.

- Cupcakes are cooked once a toothpick pricked into the middle of the cake comes out clean.

EQUIPMENT

- To complete the recipes in this book, you will need to use a selection of everyday cooking equipment and utensils, such as mixing bowls, saucepans, a sieve, knives, spoons and forks and a chopping board.

- Of course, you'll need to weigh and measure the ingredients, so you'll need a measuring cup and some kitchen scales too.

- Some of the recipes tell you to use a whisk. Ask an adult to help you use an electric whisk, or you can use a balloon whisk yourself—you'll just have to work extra hard!

- All of the recipes in this book need cupcake cases and a cupcake pan. Before starting any recipe, put the cases into the pan and preheat the oven. All other equipment that you may not have to hand are listed at the start of each recipe.

SAFETY & HYGIENE

- Before starting any cooking always wash your hands.

- Cover any cuts with a Band-aid.

- Wear an apron to protect your clothes.

- Always make sure that all the equipment you use is clean.

- If you need to use a sharp knife to cut up something hard, ask an adult to help you. Always use a chopping board.

- Remember that pans in the oven and on the stove can get very hot. Always ask an adult to turn on the oven and to get things in and out of the oven for you.

- Always ask an adult for help if you are using anything electrical—like an electric whisk.

- Be careful when heating anything in a pan on top of the stove. Keep the handle turned to one side to avoid accidentally knocking the pan.

- Keep your pets out of the kitchen while cooking.

ADULT SUPERVISION
IS REQUIRED FOR
ALL RECIPES

GETTING STARTED

MEASURING

Use scales to weigh exactly how much of each ingredient you need or use a measuring cup to measure liquids.

MIXING

Use a spoon, balloon whisk or electric hand whisk to mix the ingredients together.

DIFFERENT IDEAS

Decorate your cupcakes with flavored or colored frosting, and then add chocolate drops, candies or sugar strands.

CREATING RECIPES

Once you've made a recipe in this book a few times, think about whether you could make your own version. This way you can start to make up your own recipes. Try to think up names for the things you create!

PLEASE NOTE

The measurements given in this book are approximate. Use the same measurement conversions throughout your recipe (ounces or grams) to maintain the correct ratios. All of the recipes in this book have been created for adults to make with junior chefs and must not be attempted by an unsupervised child.

Read through each recipe to make sure you've got all the ingredients that you need before you start.

PLAIN CUPCAKES

Ingredients:
- 4 1/2 oz (125 g) all-purpose flour with raising agents
- 4 1/2 oz (125 g) butter, softened
- 4 1/2 oz (125 g) superfine sugar
- 2 large eggs
- 2–3 tablespoons whole milk

1 Preheat the oven to 350°F / 180°C.

2 Sift the flour into a bowl, followed by the butter. Use the tips of your fingers to rub the butter and flour together until the mixture becomes crumbly. Alternatively, ask an adult to use an electric whisk.

3 Add the sugar and mix it in, then stir in the eggs. Finally, add the milk to make the mixture creamy.

4 Put spoonfuls of the mixture into the cupcake cases. Bake the cupcakes for 10–15 minutes, until they are golden brown, then leave them to cool on a rack.

TOP TIP!
Make sure the oven is the required temperature before you place the cupcakes inside!

VALENTINE CUPCAKES

Extra equipment:
- piece of paper cut into a heart shape

Ingredients:
- 4 oz (100 g) all-purpose flour with raising agents
- 1 tablespoon cocoa powder
- 4 1/2 oz (125 g) butter, softened
- 4 1/2 oz (125 g) superfine sugar
- 2 large eggs
- 2–3 tablespoons whole milk

For the topping:
- confectioners' sugar

1 Preheat the oven to 350°F / 180°C.

2 Sift the flour and cocoa powder into a bowl.

3 Put the butter in the bowl. Use the tips of your fingers to rub the butter, flour and cocoa powder together until the mixture becomes crumbly. Alternatively, ask an adult to use an electric whisk.

4 Add the sugar and mix it in, then stir in the eggs.

5 Finally, add the milk to make the mixture creamy.

6 Put spoonfuls of the mixture into the cupcake cases. Bake the cupcakes for 10–15 minutes, then leave them to cool on a rack.

7 Leave the cupcakes until they are cool, then hold the heart-shaped paper cut-out over the top of the cake whilst you sprinkle over the confectioners' sugar.

TOP TIP!
Experiment with different shaped cut-outs, such as stars, moons and swirls.

VANILLA CUPCAKES

Extra equipment:
- piping bag

Ingredients:
- 8 oz (225 g) all-purpose flour with raising agents
- 3 oz (80 g) butter
- 3 oz (80 g) superfine sugar
- 1 egg
- 3–4 fl.oz (80–100 ml) whole milk

For the topping:
- 8 oz (200 g) confectioners' sugar
- 4 oz (100 g) butter, softened
- 1 teaspoon vanilla extract
- 1 tablespoon whole milk
- candy sprinkles

1 Preheat the oven to 350°F / 180°C.

2 Sift the flour into a bowl, followed by the butter.

3 Use the tips of your fingers to rub the butter and flour together until the mixture becomes crumbly.

4 Add the sugar and mix it in, then stir in the egg. Finally, add enough milk to make the mixture creamy.

5 Put spoonfuls of the mixture into the cupcake cases. Bake the cakes for 10–15 minutes, until they are golden brown, then leave them to cool on a rack.

6 Sift the confectioners' sugar into a bowl and then add the butter, vanilla extract and a tablespoon of milk. Mix well. Then place the mixture into a piping bag.

7 Pipe the topping onto the cooked cupcakes and then finish with candy sprinkles.

TOP TIP! Serve your cupcakes in saucers for a twist on your usual coffee break!

DOUBLE CHOCOLATE-CHIP CUPCAKES

Ingredients:

- 4 oz (100 g) all-purpose flour with raising agents
- 1 tablespoon cocoa powder
- 4 ½ oz (125 g) butter, softened
- 4 ½ oz (125 g) superfine sugar
- 2 large eggs
- 2–3 tablespoons whole milk
- 2 oz (50 g) chocolate chips

1 Preheat the oven to 350°F / 180°C.

2 Sift the flour and cocoa powder into a bowl.

3 Put the butter in the bowl. Use the tips of your fingers to rub the butter, flour and cocoa powder together until the mixture becomes crumbly. Alternatively, ask an adult to use an electric whisk.

4 Add the sugar and mix it in, then stir in the eggs.

5 Finally, add the milk to make the mixture creamy, followed by the chocolate chips. Stir to mix.

6 Put spoonfuls of the mixture into the cupcake cases. Bake the cupcakes for 10–15 minutes, then leave them to cool on a rack.

7 Once cool, top the cupcakes with more chocolate chips or leave plain.

TOP TIP!
Why not try white chocolate chips—yummy!

PARTY CUPCAKES

Extra equipment:
- piping bag

Ingredients:
- 4 1/2 oz (125 g) all-purpose flour with raising agents
- 4 1/2 oz (125 g) butter, softened
- 4 1/2 oz (125 g) superfine sugar
- 2 large eggs
- a few drops of vanilla extract
- 2–3 tablespoons whole milk

For the topping:
- whipped cream
- candy sprinkles

1 Preheat the oven to 350°F / 180°C.

2 Sift the flour into a bowl, followed by the butter. Use the tips of your fingers to rub the butter and flour together until the mixture becomes crumbly. Alternatively, ask an adult to use an electric whisk.

3 Add the sugar and mix it in, then stir in the eggs. Finally, add the vanilla extract and milk to make the mixture creamy.

4 Put spoonfuls of the mixture into the cupcake cases. Bake the cupcakes for 10–15 minutes, until they are golden brown, then leave them to cool on a rack.

5 Once cool, place the whipped cream into a piping bag and pipe onto the top of the cupcakes.

6 Finish with candy sprinkles.

TOP TIP!
Don't be afraid to be extravagant with the toppings! Add edible glitter, sprinkles and candles and decorate the table with party banners and streamers.

APPLE & CINNAMON SPICE CUPCAKES

Extra equipment:
• piping bag

Ingredients:
• 7 oz (190 g) all-purpose flour
• 4 oz (100 g) butter, softened
• 4 1/2 oz (125 g) superfine sugar
• 2 eggs
• 1/2 teaspoon ground cinnamon
• 1/2 teaspoon ground allspice
• 2 teaspoons baking powder
• 1/2 teaspoon baking soda
• 8 fl.oz (235 ml) apple sauce

For the topping:
• 8 oz (200 g) confectioners' sugar
• 4 oz (100 g) butter, softened
• a few drops of vanilla extract
• 1/2 teaspoon ground cinnamon

1 Preheat the oven to 350°F / 180°C.

2 Sift the flour into a bowl. In another bowl, mix together the butter and sugar until the mixture is creamy.

3 Add in the eggs and beat until smooth. Blend in the cinnamon, allspice, baking powder and baking soda.

4 Add the apple sauce and the sifted flour. Stir until just blended together.

5 Use a teaspoon to divide the mixture equally into the cupcake cases. Bake the cupcakes for 10–15 minutes, until they are golden brown, then leave them to cool on a rack.

6 For the topping, sift the confectioners' sugar into a bowl and then mix in the butter, vanilla extract and cinnamon. Add a little milk, if the mixture is too stiff, and then place in a piping bag.

7 Pipe the topping onto the cooled cupcakes and then finish with a light sprinkling of ground cinnamon.

TOP TIP!
Invest in a cake stand so you can show off all of your great cupcakes!

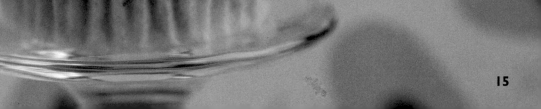

STRAWBERRY CUPCAKES

Extra equipment:
- blender
- piping bag
- sieve

Ingredients:
- 4 oz (100 g) all-purpose flour with raising agents
- 1 tablespoon cocoa powder
- 4 1/2 oz (125 g) butter
- 4 1/2 oz (125 g) superfine sugar
- 2 large eggs
- 2–3 tablespoons whole milk

For the topping:
- 7 oz (200 g) strawberries, washed, hulled and chopped
- 4 oz (100 g) butter, softened
- a few drops of vanilla extract
- 1 lb (450 g) confectioners' sugar
- candy, to decorate
- mint leaves, to decorate

1 Preheat the oven to 350°F / 180°C.

2 Sift the flour and cocoa powder into a bowl.

3 Put the butter in the bowl. Use the tips of your fingers to rub the butter, flour and cocoa powder together until the mixture becomes crumbly. Alternatively, ask an adult to use an electric whisk.

4 Add the sugar and mix it in, then stir in the eggs.

5 Finally, add the milk to make the mixture creamy.

6 Put spoonfuls of the mixture into the cupcake cases. Bake the cupcakes for 10–15 minutes, then leave them to cool on a rack.

7 For the topping, ask an adult to purée the strawberries in a blender, then sieve to remove any pips. Pour the purée into a bowl, then add the softened butter, vanilla extract and confectioners' sugar. Mix thoroughly.

8 Place into a piping bag and pipe on top of the cooled cupcakes. Finish with candies and a sprig of mint leaves.

TOP TIP! Why not decorate your cupcakes with fresh strawberries? Make sure you wash them first!

GARDEN CUPCAKES

Extra equipment:
- piping bag

Ingredients:
- 3 eggs, beaten
- 5 oz (150 g) butter, softened
- 5 oz (150 g) sugar
- 6 oz (175 g) all-purpose flour with raising agents
- a few drops of vanilla extract
- 2 drops green food coloring

For the topping:
- 5 oz (150 g) butter, softened
- 9 oz (250 g) confectioners' sugar
- a few drops of vanilla extract
- 2 drops green food coloring
- 2 teaspoons hot water
- edible flowers, to decorate

1 Preheat the oven to 375°F / 190°C.

2 Crack the eggs into a bowl and beat lightly with a fork.

3 Place the butter, sugar, flour (sifted) and vanilla extract into a large bowl. Add the beaten eggs and a couple of drops of green food coloring.

4 Beat until the mixture is light and creamy.

5 Use a teaspoon to transfer equal amounts of the mixture to the cupcake cases. Bake the cupcakes for 18–20 minutes. Leave them to cool on a rack.

6 For the topping, beat together the butter and confectioners' sugar. Once well mixed, add the vanilla extract, food coloring and water. Beat the mixture until smooth and creamy.

7 Swirl over your cupcakes and decorate with edible flowers.

TOP TIP!
If you use real flowers, remember to remove them before eating!

UNDER THE SEA CUPCAKES

Extra equipment:
• piping bag

Ingredients:
• 4 ½ oz (125 g) all-purpose flour with raising agents
• 4 ½ oz (125 g) butter, softened
• 4 ½ oz (125 g) superfine sugar
• 2 large eggs
• a few drops of vanilla extract
• 2–3 tablespoons whole milk

For the topping:
• 5 oz (140 g) butter
• 10 oz (280 g) confectioners' sugar
• 1–2 tablespoons whole milk
• a few drops of blue food coloring
• candy sprinkles

1 Preheat the oven to 350°F / 180°C.

2 Sift the flour into a bowl, followed by the butter. Use the tips of your fingers to rub the butter and flour together until the mixture becomes crumbly. Alternatively, ask an adult to use an electric whisk.

3 Add the sugar and mix it in, then stir in the eggs. Finally, add the vanilla extract and milk to make the mixture creamy.

4 Put spoonfuls of the mixture into the cupcake cases. Bake the cupcakes for 10–15 minutes, until they are golden brown, then leave them to cool on a rack.

5 For the topping, beat the butter in a large bowl until soft. Add half of the confectioners' sugar and beat until smooth. Add the remaining confectioners' sugar and one tablespoon of milk and beat the mixture until smooth.

6 Stir in the blue food coloring until well combined, then place into a piping bag.

7 Pipe the frosting on top of the cupcakes and finish with candy sprinkles.

TOP TIP!
Make a colorful array of cupcakes! Experiment with different colorings, but remember, only add a few drops!

CHOCA MOCHA CUPCAKES

Extra equipment:
- piping bag

Ingredients:
- 7 oz (200 g) superfine sugar
- 7 oz (200 g) butter, softened
- 2 teaspoons espresso-strength coffee granules
- 1 tablespoon boiling water
- 4 eggs
- 7 oz (200 g) all-purpose flour with raising agents, sifted

For the topping:
- 4 oz (100 g) butter, softened
- 6 oz (170 g) confectioners' sugar
- 2 oz (50 g) cocoa powder, sifted
- 1–2 tablespoons whole milk
- chopped nuts, to decorate

1. Preheat the oven to 350°F / 180°C.

2. Beat together the sugar and butter in a bowl.

3. Next, ask an adult to dissolve the coffee in the boiling water, then beat it into the butter mix.

4. Beat in the eggs, one at a time, then fold in the sifted flour and mix briefly until combined.

5. Put spoonfuls of the mixture into the cupcake cases. Bake the cupcakes for 20–25 minutes, until they are golden brown, then leave them to cool on a rack.

6. For the topping, place the butter in a large bowl and add half of the confectioners' sugar. Beat until smooth.

7. Then, add the remaining confectioners' sugar, cocoa powder and one tablespoon of milk and beat until creamy. Beat in more milk if necessary to loosen the frosting.

8. Spoon or pipe the frosting onto the top of the cupcakes and sprinkle with chopped nuts to finish.

TOP TIP! For an extra treat, why not top with two different flavored icings? Experiment!

CELEBRATION CUPCAKES

TOP TIP!
Add popping candy to the topping for a tongue-tingling twist!

MAKES 12

Ingredients:

- 4 ¹/₂ oz (125 g) all-purpose flour with raising agents
- 4 ¹/₂ oz (125 g) butter, softened
- 4 ¹/₂ oz (125 g) superfine sugar
- 2 eggs
- a few drops of vanilla extract
- 2–3 tablespoons whole milk

For the topping:

- 5 oz (140 g) butter, softened
- 10 oz (280 g) confectioners' sugar
- 1–2 tablespoons whole milk
- a few drops of yellow food coloring
- candy sprinkles
- gold or silver candy balls

1 Preheat the oven to 350°F / 180°C.

2 Sift the flour into a bowl, followed by the butter. Use the tips of your fingers to rub the butter and flour together until the mixture becomes crumbly. Alternatively, ask an adult to use an electric whisk.

3 Add the sugar and mix it in, then stir in the eggs.

4 Finally, add the vanilla extract and milk to make the mixture creamy.

5 Put spoonfuls of the mixture into the cupcake cases. Bake the cupcakes for 10–15 minutes, until they are golden brown, then leave them to cool on a rack.

6 For the topping, place the softened butter in a large bowl and add half of the confectioners' sugar. Beat until smooth.

7 Add the remaining confectioners' sugar and one tablespoon of milk and beat the mixture until creamy and smooth. Beat in more milk if necessary to loosen the frosting mixture.

8 Stir in the yellow food coloring until well combined.

9 Place the frosting in a piping bag and pipe on top of the cupcakes. Finish with candy sprinkles and gold or silver balls—perfect for a celebration!

CHOCOLATE MINT CUPCAKES

Extra equipment:
- piping bag

Ingredients:
- 2 oz (60 g) bittersweet chocolate
- 5 fl.oz (150 ml) water
- 2 eggs
- 5 oz (150 g) brown sugar
- 1/4 teaspoon peppermint flavoring
- 4 oz (90 g) butter, softened
- 4 oz (125 g) all-purpose flour with raising agents
- 2 tablespoons cocoa powder
- 1 oz (30 g) ground almonds

For the topping:
- 5 oz (150 g) butter, softened
- 9 oz (250 g) confectioners' sugar
- a few drops of peppermint flavoring
- 2 drops green food coloring
- 2 teaspoons hot water

1 Preheat the oven to 350°F / 180°C.

2 Place the chocolate and water into a small saucepan. Ask an adult to stir over a low heat until melted and smooth. Set aside.

3 Place the eggs, brown sugar, peppermint flavoring and softened butter in a large mixing bowl. Beat the ingredients until light and fluffy.

4 Sift in the flour and cocoa powder. Add the ground almonds. Stir well to combine. Add the warm chocolate to the mixture and stir until just combined.

5 Use a teaspoon to transfer equal amounts of the mixture to the cupcake cases. Bake the cupcakes for about 18–20 minutes. Leave them to cool on a rack.

6 For the topping, beat together the butter and confectioners' sugar. Once well mixed, add the peppermint flavoring, food coloring and hot water. Beat until smooth and creamy.

7 Then, place the topping mixture into a piping bag and swirl over your cupcakes.

TOP TIP!
Add 2 oz (50 g) chocolate chips in place of the almonds for a nice variation!

21

CUPCAKE NESTS

Extra equipment:
- piping bag

Ingredients:
- 9 oz (250 g) all-purpose flour, sifted
- 14 oz (400 g) superfine sugar
- ½ teaspoon baking powder
- 1 teaspoon baking soda
- 4 oz (100 g) butter
- 4 oz (100 g) bittersweet chocolate
- 6 fl.oz (180 ml) water
- 2 eggs
- 6 fl.oz (180 ml) whole milk
- a few drops of vanilla extract

For the topping:
- 5 oz (150 g) butter, softened
- 9 oz (250 g) confectioners' sugar
- 2 tablespoons cocoa powder
- chocolate eggs

1 Preheat the oven to 350°F / 180°C.

2 Put the sifted flour, sugar, baking powder, baking soda and butter in a large bowl. Mix together.

3 Next, ask an adult to melt the bittersweet chocolate in a heatproof bowl over a pan of hot water. Make sure the water doesn't touch the bottom of the bowl.

4 Add the water, eggs, milk, vanilla extract and melted chocolate to the flour mixture.

5 Beat together until thoroughly mixed.

6 Use a teaspoon to transfer equal amounts of the mixture to the cupcake cases. Bake the cupcakes for 20–25 minutes. Leave them to cool on a rack.

7 For the topping, beat together the butter and confectioners' sugar. Combine the cocoa powder with a little water, and add to the mixture. Beat until smooth and creamy.

8 Place the topping into a piping bag and pipe onto each cupcake. Top with a chocolate egg.

TOP TIP! Purchase some decorative edible flowers for a nice seasonal display.

ORANGE CREAM CUPCAKES

Ingredients:
- 7 oz (190 g) all-purpose flour
- ½ teaspoon baking powder
- 4 oz (100 g) butter
- 7 oz (200 g) superfine sugar
- 2 eggs
- 1 tablespoon orange juice
- ½ tablespoon orange zest
- 6 fl.oz (170 ml) whole milk

For the topping:
- 4 oz (100 g) cream cheese
- 1 oz (25 g) butter
- 1 teaspoon orange zest
- ½ teaspoon vanilla extract
- 4 ½ oz (120 g) confectioners' sugar
- edible glitter

1 Preheat the oven to 350°F / 180°C.

2 Sift the flour and baking powder into a bowl and set aside.

3 In another bowl, beat the butter and sugar together, until light and fluffy. Alternatively, ask an adult to use an electric whisk on a medium speed for 2–3 minutes.

4 Add the eggs to the butter and sugar mixture, one at a time, beating well after each one.

5 Now beat in the orange juice and zest. Next, mix in the flour and baking powder and the milk, alternating a little at a time. Stir until just combined.

6 Use a teaspoon to transfer equal amounts of the mixture to the cupcake cases. Bake the cupcakes for 17–19 minutes. Leave them to cool on a rack.

7 For the topping, beat together the cream cheese and butter until light and creamy. Add in the orange zest, vanilla extract and confectioners' sugar, beating until smooth.

8 Swirl over your cupcakes and add a sprinkling of edible glitter.

TOP TIP!
Place your cupcakes in an airtight container to keep them as fresh as possible.

23

HALLOWEEN CUPCAKES

TOP TIP!
Try out different spooky decorations—skeletons, witches' hats or bats!

MAKES 12

Extra equipment:
- frosting syringe

Ingredients:
- 4 ¹/₂ oz (125 g) all-purpose flour with raising agents
- 4 ¹/₂ oz (125 g) butter, softened
- 4 ¹/₂ oz (125 g) superfine sugar
- 2 eggs
- a few drops of vanilla extract
- 2–3 tablespoons whole milk

For the topping:
- 5 oz (140 g) butter, softened
- 10 oz (280 g) confectioners' sugar
- 1–2 tablespoons whole milk
- a few drops of orange food coloring

For the spider:
- 1 egg white
- 4 oz (100 g) confectioners' sugar
- a few drops of black food coloring

1 Preheat the oven to 350°F / 180°C.

2 Sift the flour into a bowl, followed by the butter. Use the tips of your fingers to rub the butter and flour together until the mixture becomes crumbly. Alternatively, ask an adult to use an electric whisk. Add the sugar and mix it in, then stir in the eggs. Finally, add the vanilla extract and milk to make the mixture creamy.

3 Put spoonfuls of the mixture into the cupcake cases. Bake the cupcakes for 10–15 minutes, until they are golden brown, then leave them to cool on a rack.

4 For the topping, place the butter in a large bowl and add half the confectioners' sugar.

5 Beat until smooth. Add the remaining confectioners' sugar and one tablespoon of the milk and beat the mixture until creamy and smooth. Beat in more milk if necessary to loosen the frosting. Stir in the orange food coloring until well combined, then spread the topping onto the top of each cupcake.

6 To make the spider: beat an egg white in a bowl. Sift the confectioners' sugar into the bowl. Beat the mixture until the frosting becomes smooth and thick. Add a few drops of black food coloring, then spoon the frosting into a frosting syringe. Carefully pipe your spider decoration onto the cupcakes. Ask an adult to run a knife carefully along the spider to add texture.

FLOWER PETAL CUPCAKES

Extra equipment:
- piping bag
- rolling pin

Ingredients:
- 4 1/2 oz (125 g) all-purpose flour with raising agents
- 4 1/2 oz (125 g) butter, softened
- 4 1/2 oz (125 g) superfine sugar
- 2 eggs
- a few drops of vanilla extract
- 2–3 tablespoons whole milk

For the topping:
- 5 oz (140 g) butter, softened
- 10 oz (280 g) confectioners' sugar
- 1–2 tablespoons whole milk
- a few drops of pink food coloring
- ready-to-use frosting
- candies, to decorate

1 Preheat the oven to 350°F / 180°C.

2 Sift the flour into a bowl, followed by the butter. Use the tips of your fingers to rub the butter and flour together until the mixture becomes crumbly. Alternatively, ask an adult to use an electric whisk. Add the sugar and mix it in, then stir in the eggs. Finally, add the vanilla extract and milk to make the mixture creamy.

3 Put spoonfuls of the mixture into the cupcake cases. Bake the cupcakes for 10–15 minutes, until they are golden brown, then leave them to cool on a rack.

4 For the topping, place the butter in a large bowl and add half of the confectioners' sugar. Beat until smooth.

5 Add the remaining confectioners' sugar and one tablespoon of milk and beat the mixture until creamy and smooth. Beat in more milk if necessary to loosen the frosting. Place in a piping bag and pipe on top of the cupcakes.

6 Next, knead a few drops of food coloring (more or less depending on how pink you would like the petals to be) into a section of the ready-to-use frosting. Once the color is even, roll out the frosting. Ask an adult to cut the frosting into petal shapes, using a sharp knife. Run the knife lightly over each petal to add texture. Form the petals together so they make a flower and curl the outside of the petals upwards. Place the petals onto each cupcake and top with a candy.

TOP TIP! Make smaller petals and flowers so you can add more than one to each cake!

25

WINTER SNOW CUPCAKES

Extra equipment:
- rolling pin

Ingredients:
- 3 eggs
- 5 oz (150 g) butter, softened
- 5 oz (150 g) sugar
- 6 oz (175 g) all-purpose flour with raising agents, sifted
- a few drops of vanilla extract

For the topping:
- a few drops of blue food coloring
- ready-to-use frosting

1 Preheat the oven to 350°F / 180°C.

2 Crack the eggs into a bowl and beat lightly with a fork. Add the beaten eggs to a large bowl containing the butter, sugar, sifted flour and vanilla extract.

3 Beat until the mixture is light and creamy.

4 Use a teaspoon to transfer equal amounts of the mixture to the cupcake cases. Bake the cupcakes for 18–20 minutes. Leave them to cool on a rack.

5 Knead a couple of drops of food coloring into half of the ready-to-use frosting. When the color is even, roll out the icing and cut out blue snowflake shapes to cover each cupcake.

6 Cut out smaller snowflake shapes from the remaining ready-to-use frosting and place these on top of the blue frosting base layer.

TOP TIP!
You could use marzipan instead of frosting for the topping!

GINGERBREAD CUPCAKES

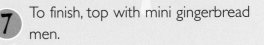

Extra equipment:
- piping bag

Ingredients:
- 2 oz (50 g) all-purpose flour with raising agents
- 2 oz (50 g) all-purpose flour
- 1/4 teaspoon baking soda
- 1 teaspoon ground ginger
- 1/2 teaspoon ground cinnamon
- 1/4 teaspoon ground nutmeg
- 4 oz (100 g) brown sugar
- 1 egg
- 4 oz (100 g) butter, softened
- 2–3 tablespoons whole milk
- 2 tablespoons light corn syrup

For the topping:
- 4 oz (100 g) cream cheese
- 1 oz (25 g) butter
- 1/2 teaspoon vanilla extract
- 4 1/2 oz (120 g) confectioners' sugar
- mini gingerbread men

1 Preheat the oven to 350°F / 180°C.

2 Sift the flours, baking soda, ginger, cinnamon and nutmeg into a large bowl.

3 Add the remaining ingredients. Mix together with a wooden spoon, or alternatively, ask an adult to use an electric whisk.

4 Put spoonfuls of the mixture into the cupcake cases. Bake the cupcakes for 10–15 minutes, until they are golden brown, then leave them to cool on a rack.

5 For the topping, beat together the cream cheese and butter.

6 Add in the vanilla extract and confectioners' sugar, beating until smooth. Place in a piping bag and pipe onto the top of each cupcake.

7 To finish, top with mini gingerbread men.

TOP TIP!
If you have the time, why not make your own gingerbread men!

27

CREAMY CHOCOLATE CUPCAKES

Extra equipment:
- piping bag

Ingredients:
- 4 oz (100 g) all-purpose flour with raising agents
- 1 tablespoon cocoa powder
- 4 1/2 oz (125 g) butter, softened
- 4 1/2 oz (125 g) superfine sugar
- 2 large eggs
- 2–3 tablespoons whole milk

For the topping:
- whipped cream
- a few drops of vanilla extract

1 Preheat the oven to 350°F / 180°C.

2 Sift the flour and cocoa powder into a bowl.

3 Put the butter in the bowl. Use the tips of your fingers to rub the butter, flour and cocoa powder together until the mixture becomes crumbly. Alternatively, ask an adult to use an electric whisk.

4 Add the sugar and mix it in, then stir in the eggs.

5 Finally, add the milk to make the mixture creamy.

6 Put spoonfuls of the mixture into the cupcake cases. Bake the cupcakes for 10–15 minutes, then leave them to cool on a rack.

7 Once cool, place the whipped cream, mixed with the vanilla extract, into a piping bag and pipe onto the top of the cupcakes.

TOP TIP!
Try using different flavored extracts in the creamy topping.

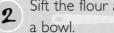

28

BANOFFEE CUPCAKES

Extra equipment:
- piping bag

Ingredients:
- 4 oz (100 g) butter, softened
- 2 oz (50 g) superfine sugar
- 2 oz (60 g) dulce de leche or milk caramel
- 2 eggs, lightly beaten
- 2 small ripe bananas
- 4 1/2 oz (120 g) all-purpose flour with raising agents, sifted
- 1/2 tsp baking powder

For the topping:
- whipped cream
- soft toffee, broken into pieces, to decorate

1 Preheat the oven to 350°F / 180°C.

2 Place the butter in a bowl, then beat in the sugar and the dulce de leche until smooth and creamy.

3 Beat in the eggs, a quarter at a time, making sure each lot is well mixed in before adding the next.

4 Peel and thoroughly mash the bananas before adding to the mixture. Stir in well.

5 Finally, fold in the sifted flour and baking powder and beat for a couple of seconds to combine.

6 Put spoonfuls of the mixture into the cupcake cases. Bake the cupcakes for 10–15 minutes, then leave them to cool on a rack.

7 Once cool, place the whipped cream into a piping bag and pipe onto the top of the cupcakes.

8 Finish off with a sprinkling of broken toffee pieces.

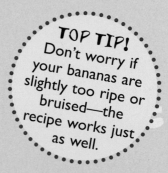

TOP TIP!
Don't worry if your bananas are slightly too ripe or bruised—the recipe works just as well.

29

PRETTY IN PINK CUPCAKES

Ingredients:

- 4 ¹/₂ oz (125 g) all-purpose flour with raising agents
- 4 ¹/₂ oz (125 g) butter, softened
- 4 ¹/₂ oz (125 g) superfine sugar
- 2 large eggs
- 2–3 tablespoons whole milk

For the topping:

- 5 oz (140 g) butter, softened
- 10 oz (280 g) confectioners' sugar
- 1–2 tablespoons whole milk
- a few drops of pink food coloring
- candy sprinkles

1 Preheat the oven to 350°F / 180°C.

2 Sift the flour into a bowl, followed by the butter. Use the tips of your fingers to rub the butter and flour together until the mixture becomes crumbly. Alternatively, ask an adult to use an electric whisk.

3 Add the sugar and mix it in, then stir in the eggs.

4 Finally, add the milk to make the mixture creamy.

5 Put spoonfuls of the mixture into the cupcake cases. Bake the cupcakes for 10–15 minutes, until they are golden brown, then leave them to cool on a rack.

6 For the topping, place the butter in a large bowl and add half of the confectioners' sugar. Beat until smooth. Add the remaining confectioners' sugar and one tablespoon of the milk and beat the mixture until creamy and smooth. Beat in more milk if necessary to loosen the frosting.

7 Stir in the pink food coloring until well combined, then swirl onto the top of each cupcake. Top with candy sprinkles to finish.

TOP TIP! These cupcakes will go down brilliantly at a party. For added "wow" factor, display them with a pink feather boa backdrop!

SPRING CUPCAKES

Extra equipment:
- piping bag with a thin nozzle
- rolling pin

Ingredients:
- 4 ½ oz (125 g) all-purpose flour with raising agents
- 4 ½ oz (125 g) butter, softened
- 4 ½ oz (125 g) superfine sugar
- 2 large eggs
- 2–3 tablespoons whole milk

For the topping:
- 5 oz (140 g) butter, softened
- 10 oz (280 g) confectioners' sugar
- 1–2 tablespoons whole milk
- a few drops of green food coloring
- ready-to-use frosting
- a few drops of yellow food coloring

1 Preheat the oven to 350°F / 180°C.

2 Sift the flour into a bowl, followed by the butter. Use the tips of your fingers to rub the butter and flour together until the mixture becomes crumbly. Alternatively, ask an adult to use an electric whisk. Add the sugar and mix it in, then stir in the eggs. Finally, add the milk to make the mixture creamy.

3 Put spoonfuls of the mixture into the cupcake cases. Bake the cupcakes for 10–15 minutes, until they are golden brown, then leave them to cool on a rack.

4 For the topping, place the butter in a large bowl and add half of the confectioners' sugar. Beat until smooth.

5 Add the remaining confectioners' sugar and one tablespoon of the milk and beat the mixture until creamy and smooth. Beat in more milk if necessary to loosen the frosting. Add the green food coloring and mix well, before placing the mixture into a piping bag with a thin nozzle. Next, pipe the topping onto the cupcakes, lifting the nozzle upwards to create a grass-like effect for each strand.

6 Next, roll the ready-to-use frosting, then ask an adult to cut it into petal shapes, using a sharp knife. Form the petals together so they make a flower and place onto each cupcake.

7 Add yellow food coloring to the remaining icing. Cut into small circles and place on top of the petals to finish.

TOP TIP!
Make some little frosting bugs to go in your grass! Just follow the spider instructions on page 24.

COFFEE & WALNUT CUPCAKES

Extra equipment:
- piping bag

Ingredients:
- 7 oz (200 g) superfine sugar
- 7 oz (200 g) butter, softened
- 2 teaspoons espresso-strength coffee granules
- 1 tablespoon boiling water
- 4 eggs
- 7 oz (200 g) all-purpose flour with raising agents, sifted

For the topping:
- 4 1/2 oz (125 g) mascarpone
- 4 1/2 oz (125 g) butter, softened
- 1/4 teaspoon grated lemon zest
- 12 oz (350 g) confectioners' sugar, sifted
- walnut halves, to decorate

1 Preheat the oven to 350°F / 180°C.

2 Beat together the sugar and butter in a bowl.

3 Next, ask an adult to dissolve the coffee in the boiling water, then beat it into the butter mix.

4 Beat in the eggs, one at a time, then fold in the sifted flour and mix briefly until combined.

5 Put spoonfuls of the mixture into the cupcake cases. Bake the cupcakes for 20–25 minutes, until they are golden brown, then leave them to cool on a rack.

6 For the topping, put the mascarpone, butter and lemon zest into a bowl and beat together. Add the confectioners' sugar, about one-third at a time, working in completely before adding the next batch.

7 Place the topping mixture into a piping bag and swirl onto the top of the cupcakes.

8 Finish each cake with a walnut half.

TOP TIP!
Try different nuts, such as pecans, Brazil nuts and almonds.

RASPBERRY CHOCOLATE CUPCAKES

Extra equipment:
- piping bag

Ingredients:
- 2 oz (50 g) bittersweet chocolate
- 4 fl.oz (120 ml) water
- 2 eggs
- 8 oz (225 g) brown sugar
- 4 oz (100 g) butter, softened
- 4 oz (100 g) all-purpose flour with raising agents
- 2 tablespoons cocoa powder
- 2 oz (50 g) ground almonds
- 4 oz (100 g) frozen raspberries

For the topping:
- 5 oz (150 g) butter, softened
- 9 oz (250 g) confectioners' sugar
- a few drops of vanilla extract
- 3 drops pink food coloring
- 2 tablespoons hot water
- chocolate stars, to decorate

1 Preheat the oven to 350°F / 180°C.

2 Place the bittersweet chocolate and water into a small saucepan. Stir over a low heat until melted and smooth. Set aside to cool.

3 Place the eggs, brown sugar and butter in a large mixing bowl. Beat until just combined.

4 Sift in the all-purpose flour with raising agents and cocoa powder, and add in the ground almonds. Stir well to combine.

5 Add the warm chocolate to the mixture and stir until just combined.

6 Use a teaspoon to transfer equal amounts of the mixture to the cupcake cases, half filling each case. Place a couple of raspberries in the middle, and then top with the remaining mixture. Bake the cupcakes for about 20–25 minutes. Leave to cool on a rack.

7 For the topping, beat together the butter and confectioners' sugar. Once well mixed, add the vanilla extract, food coloring and water. Beat until smooth.

8 Place the topping in a piping bag and swirl over your cupcakes. Decorate with chocolate stars to finish.

TOP TIP!
Top with fresh raspberries for a summertime treat!

33

CHRISTMAS CUPCAKES

Extra equipment:
- rolling pin
- cookie cutters, various shapes

Ingredients:
- 4 oz (100 g) all-purpose flour with raising agents
- 1 tablespoon cocoa powder
- 4 1/2 oz (125 g) butter, softened
- 4 1/2 oz (125 g) superfine sugar
- 2 large eggs
- 2–3 tablespoons whole milk

For the topping:
- ready-to-use frosting
- red food coloring
- green food coloring
- candies or silver balls

1 Preheat the oven to 350°F / 180°C.

2 Sift the flour and cocoa powder into a bowl, followed by the butter. Use the tips of your fingers to rub the butter, flour and cocoa powder together until the mixture becomes crumbly.

3 Add the sugar and mix it in, then stir in the eggs.

4 Finally, add the milk to make the mixture creamy.

5 Put spoonfuls of the mixture into the cupcake cases. Bake the cupcakes for 10–15 minutes, then leave them to cool on a rack.

6 For the topping, roll out some of the ready-to-use frosting and cut out shapes with cookie cutters. Lay over a few of the cupcakes.

7 Next, knead a couple of drops of red food coloring into some of the remaining frosting. When the color is even, roll out the frosting and cut out festive shapes. Repeat the process, this time with the green food coloring.

8 Lay the different shapes over the tops of the rest of the cupcakes and finish with candies or silver balls.

TOP TIP!
Pipe extra decorations onto the top of the cupcakes with frosting, using a piping bag with a thin nozzle.

LEMON CURD CUPCAKES

Extra equipment:
• piping bag

Ingredients:
• 4 oz (100 g) butter, softened
• 4 oz (100 g) cream cheese
• 2 teaspoons grated lemon rind
• 5 oz (150 g) superfine sugar
• 2 eggs
• 2 oz (50 g) all-purpose flour
• 2 oz (50 g) all-purpose flour
  with raising agents

For the topping:
• 4 oz (100 g) lemon curd
• confectioners' sugar

1 Preheat the oven to 350°F / 180°C.

2 Place the butter, cream cheese, lemon rind, sugar, and eggs into a large bowl. Beat until the mixture is light and creamy.

3 Sift in the all-purpose flour and all-purpose flour with raising agents. Add them gradually to the mixture and beat until just combined.

4 Use a teaspoon to transfer equal amounts of the mixture to the cupcake cases. Bake the cupcakes for 20 minutes or until golden brown. Leave them to cool on a rack.

5 For the topping, place the lemon curd in a piping bag. Pipe onto the top of each cupcake and then finish with a light sprinkling of confectioners' sugar.

TOP TIP!
These cupcakes taste great even without the topping!

35

BUTTERFLY CUPCAKES

TOP TIP!
Be extra careful when placing the delicate butterfly wings!

Ingredients:
- 4 oz (100 g) butter
- 4 oz (100 g) superfine sugar
- 2 eggs
- 4 oz (100 g) all-purpose flour
  with raising agents

For the topping:
- 3 oz (80 g) butter
- 5 oz (150 g) confectioners' sugar
- 1–2 tablespoons whole milk

1 Preheat the oven to 350°F / 180°C.

2 Put the butter and sugar into a mixing bowl. Use a wooden spoon to beat them together until the mixture is fluffy and very pale in color. Beat in the eggs, one at a time, adding a tablespoon of flour with each one. Sift the rest of the flour into the bowl. Use a tablespoon to mix the ingredients gently. This will make sure your mixture stays nice and fluffy.

3 Use a teaspoon to transfer equal amounts of the mixture to the cupcake cases. Bake the buns for 20–25 minutes or until they are well risen and golden brown. Leave them to cool on a rack.

4 To make the butterfly wings, cut a slice from the top of each cake. Now cut each slice in half.

5 To make the buttercream topping, use a wooden spoon or an electric mixer to beat the butter in a large bowl until it is soft. Sift half of the confectioners' sugar into the bowl, and then beat it with the butter until the mixture is smooth. Then, sift the rest of the confectioners' sugar into the bowl and add one tablespoon of milk. Beat the mixture until it is smooth and creamy.

6 Place a little buttercream frosting on top of each bun. Now, gently push two of the halved slices into the frosting on each bun at an angle to form pretty butterfly wings.

MARSHMALLOW CUPCAKES

Extra equipment:
• piping bag

Ingredients:
• 4 1/2 oz (125 g) all-purpose flour with raising agents
• 4 1/2 oz (125 g) butter, softened
• 4 1/2 oz (125 g) superfine sugar
• 2 large eggs
• 2–3 tablespoons whole milk
• 12 large pink marshmallows

For the topping:
• 7 oz (200 g) pink marshmallows
• 1 lb (450 g) butter, softened
• 1 lb (450 g) confectioners' sugar
• a few drops of vanilla extract
• mini marshmallows, to decorate
• candy sprinkles

1 Preheat the oven to 350°F / 180°C.

2 Sift the flour into a bowl, followed by the butter. Use the tips of your fingers to rub the butter and flour together until the mixture becomes crumbly. Alternatively, ask an adult to use an electric whisk.

3 Add the sugar and mix it in, then stir in the eggs. Finally, add the milk to make the mixture creamy.

4 Put spoonfuls of the mixture into the cupcake cases, half filling each case. Place a marshmallow into the middle, then top with the remaining mixture. Bake the cupcakes for 15–20 minutes, until they are golden brown, then leave them to cool on a rack.

5 For the topping, add the pink marshmallows and butter to a pan and ask an adult to heat for a couple of minutes, then leave to cool.

6 Next, sift the confectioners' sugar into the mixture and add the vanilla extract. Stir well to combine.

7 Place the mixture into a piping bag and pipe onto each of the cupcakes. Top with mini marshmallows and candy sprinkles to finish.

TOP TIP!
If you have any marshmallows left over, place them on top of a hot chocolate with a big dollop of whipped cream— yummy!

CARROT CUPCAKES

Ingredients:
- 4 ¹/₂ oz (125 g) wholewheat flour
- 4 ¹/₂ oz (125 g) all-purpose flour
- 4 oz (100 g) raisins
- 2 oz (50 g) brown sugar
- 1 teaspoon baking powder
- 8 fl.oz (225 ml) whole milk
- 4 oz (100 g) shredded carrot
- 2 eggs
- 2 oz (50 g) butter, melted

For the topping:
- 4 oz (100 g) cream cheese
- 1 oz (25 g) butter
- ¹/₂ teaspoon vanilla extract
- 4 ¹/₂ oz (120 g) confectioners' sugar
- 2 oz (50 g) nuts, chopped (your favorite variety)
- marzipan carrots, to decorate

1 Preheat the oven to 350°F / 180°C.

2 Sift the wholewheat flour and all-purpose flour into a bowl, along with the raisins, sugar and baking powder. Stir them all together with a wooden spoon until they are well mixed.

3 Put the remaining ingredients in a small bowl and mix together. Then, add to the larger bowl and mix together.

4 Use a teaspoon to divide the mixture equally into the cupcake cases. Bake the cupcakes for 15 minutes, then leave them in the pan to cool.

5 For the topping, beat together the cream cheese and butter until light and creamy.

6 Add in the vanilla extract and confectioners' sugar, beating until smooth.

7 Swirl over your cupcakes and add a sprinkling of chopped nuts and a marzipan carrot.

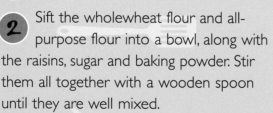

TOP TIP!
Experiment with cupcake cases. Keep an eye out for unusual designs in kitchen accessory and homeware stores.

COCONUT CUPCAKES

Ingredients:
- 8 oz (225 g) all-purpose flour with raising agents
- 3 oz (75 g) butter
- 3 oz (75 g) superfine sugar
- 1 egg
- 2–4 fl.oz (75–100 ml) whole milk

For the topping:
- whipped cream
- pink coconut ice, grated

1 Preheat the oven to 350°F / 180°C.

2 Sift the flour into a bowl, followed by the butter. Use the tips of your fingers to rub the butter and flour together until the mixture becomes crumbly.

3 Add the sugar and stir in the egg.

4 Finally, add enough milk to make the mixture creamy.

5 Put spoonfuls of the mixture into the cupcake cases. Bake the cupcakes for 10–15 minutes, then leave them to cool on a rack.

6 Decorate them with a generous swirl of freshly whipped cream and cover with grated pink coconut ice.

TOP TIP!
Place a plate underneath each cupcake whilst you sprinkle the coconut.

COLORFUL CUPCAKES

Extra equipment:
- rolling pin
- cookie cutters

Ingredients:
- 8 oz (225 g) all-purpose flour with raising agents
- 3 oz (80 g) butter
- 3 oz (80 g) superfine sugar
- 1 egg
- 3–4 fl.oz (75–100 ml) whole milk

For the topping:
- ready-to-use frosting
- food coloring

1. Preheat the oven to 350°F / 180°C.

2. Sift the flour into a bowl, followed by the butter. Use your fingertips to rub the butter and flour together until the mixture becomes crumbly.

3. Add the sugar and mix it in, then stir in the egg. Finally, add enough milk to make the mixture creamy.

4. Put spoonfuls of the mixture into the cupcake cases. Bake the cupcakes for 10–15 minutes, until they are golden brown, then leave them to cool.

5. For the decorative topping, knead a couple of drops of food coloring into some of the frosting. When the color is even, roll out the frosting and cut out shapes, either with a cookie cutter or ask an adult to use a sharp knife. Lay the different shapes over the tops of the cupcakes.

6. Repeat the process, with different food colorings and frosting shapes.

TOP TIP!
Experiment with different shapes and colors. Try to make each cupcake look different!

CHOC-CHIP COOKIE CUPCAKES

Extra equipment:
- rolling pin
- mini cookie cutters
- piping bag

Ingredients:
- as Plain Cupcakes, page 10

For the cookies:
- 12 oz (350 g) all-purpose flour
- 1 teaspoon baking soda
- 8 oz (225 g) butter
- 6 ½ oz (175 g) superfine sugar
- 6 ½ oz (175 g) soft brown sugar
- a few drops of vanilla extract
- 2 eggs
- 4 oz (100 g) chocolate chips

For the topping:
- 5 oz (140 g) butter, softened
- 10 oz (280 g) confectioners' sugar
- 1–2 tablespoons whole milk
- chocolate chips, to decorate

1 Preheat the oven to 350°F / 180°C.

2 Follow the plain cupcake recipe on page 10, but also add chocolate chips to the mixture before placing the mixture into the cupcake cases.

3 Whilst the cupcakes are cooking, make the cookies. First, combine the flour and baking soda in a bowl.

4 In another bowl, combine the butter, sugar, brown sugar and vanilla extract until creamy. Beat in the eggs.

5 Gradually beat in the flour mixture and stir in the chocolate chips.

6 Then, roll the mixture out and use a cookie cutter to cut out mini cookie shapes. Lay on a baking sheet, spaced widely apart and bake for 9–11 minutes.

7 For the topping, place the butter in a large bowl and add half of the confectioners' sugar. Beat until smooth. Add the remaining confectioners' sugar and one tablespoon of the milk and beat the mixture until creamy and smooth. Beat in more milk if necessary to loosen the frosting.

8 Add the topping to a piping bag and pipe onto the top of each cooled cupcake. Top with a sprinkle of chocolate chips and a mini cookie.

TOP TIP! Serve with a cup of hot cocoa!

CITRUS CUPCAKES

Extra equipment:
• piping bag

Ingredients:
• 4 ¹/₂ oz (125 g) butter
• 5 oz (150 g) superfine sugar
• zest and juice of 1 orange
• zest and juice of 1 lemon
• 6 oz (180 g) all-purpose flour
  with raising agents
• 2 eggs, beaten

For the topping:
• ¹/₂ teaspoon orange zest
• ¹/₂ teaspoon lemon zest
• ¹/₂ teaspoon vanilla extract
• 4 oz (100 g) whipped cream
• candied orange segments,
  to decorate

1 Preheat the oven to 350°F / 180°C.

2 Put the butter and sugar in a bowl. Beat together with a wooden spoon, or alternatively, ask an adult to use an electric whisk.

3 Next, add the zest of the orange and lemon, and mix in well.

4 Then, sift one third of the flour, along with the eggs and 1¹/₂ tablespoons of lemon juice and 1¹/₂ tablespoons of orange juice.

5 Mix, then sift another third of flour, then mix, and then sift in the final third.

6 Use a teaspoon to divide the mixture equally into the cupcake cases. Bake the cupcakes for 15 minutes, then leave them in the tray to cool.

7 For the topping, add the orange and lemon zest and vanilla extract to the whipped cream, beating until smooth.

8 Place in a piping bag and pipe onto the top of each cupcake. Finish each cupcake with a candied orange segment.

TOP TIP!
Dig into these citrus cakes with a big glass of freshly-squeezed orange juice!

CHOCOLATE ORANGE CUPCAKES

Extra equipment:
- piping bag

Ingredients:
- 4 oz (100 g) butter
- 4 ½ oz (125 g) bittersweet chocolate, broken into small squares
- 5 oz (135 g) superfine sugar
- 2 eggs, lightly beaten
- 1 tablespoon sour cream
- ¼ teaspoon vanilla extract
- finely grated zest of 1 orange
- 1 oz (25 g) ground almonds
- 4 oz (100 g) all-purpose flour with raising agents
- 1 tablespoon cocoa powder

For the topping:
- 4 oz (100 g) cream cheese
- 1 oz (25 g) butter
- 1 teaspoon orange zest
- ½ teaspoon vanilla extract
- 4 ½ oz (120 g) confectioners' sugar

1 Preheat the oven to 350°F / 180°C.

2 Put the butter in a small saucepan and ask an adult to stir over a low heat until melted and smooth. Next, remove from the stove and stand for 2 minutes.

3 Add the chocolate and leave to stand for a further 2 minutes. Stir until smooth, then add the sugar and mix in well.

4 Ask an adult to beat in the eggs, a little at a time, making sure everything is well mixed before adding the next.

5 Beat in the sour cream, vanilla extract, orange zest, and ground almonds, then sift in the flour and cocoa powder. Mix until combined.

6 Use a teaspoon to transfer equal amounts of the mixture to the cupcake cases. Bake the cupcakes for about 15–20 minutes. Leave them to cool on a rack.

7 For the topping, beat together the cream cheese and butter. Add in the orange zest, vanilla extract and confectioners' sugar, beating until smooth.

8 Place in a piping bag and pipe onto the top of each cupcake.

TOP TIP!
Finish these fab cupcakes with a sprinkling of orange zest and chopped walnuts.

43

JELLY CUPCAKES

Ingredients:
- 4 ¹/₂ oz (125 g) all-purpose flour with raising agents
- 4 ¹/₂ oz (125 g) butter, softened
- 4 ¹/₂ oz (125 g) superfine sugar
- 2 large eggs
- 2–3 tablespoons whole milk
- 4 oz (100 g) jelly

For the topping:
- 4 oz (100 g) confectioners' sugar
- 1–2 tablespoons hot water
- a few drops of pink food coloring
- 12 jelly beans

1 Preheat the oven to 350°F / 180°C.

2 Sift the flour into a bowl, followed by the butter. Use the tips of your fingers to rub the butter and flour together until the mixture becomes crumbly. Alternatively, ask an adult to use an electric whisk.

3 Add the sugar and mix it in, then stir in the eggs.

4 Finally, add the milk to make the mixture creamy.

5 Put spoonfuls of the mixture into the cupcake cases, filling them halfway. Drop a teaspoonful of jelly on top of the mixture and then cover with the remaining mixture.

6 Bake the cupcakes for 10–15 minutes, until they are golden brown, then leave them to cool on a rack.

7 To make the topping, sift the confectioners' sugar into a bowl and add 1–2 tablespoons of hot water. Mix until you have a thick paste.

8 Add one or two drops of pink food coloring. Once well mixed, spoon the pink frosting onto each cupcake and top with a jelly bean.

TOP TIP!
Add more than one jelly bean to each cupcake if you like!

44

PIRATE CUPCAKES

Extra equipment:
- frosting syringe

Ingredients:
- 4 ¹/₂ oz (125 g) all-purpose flour with raising agents
- 4 ¹/₂ oz (125 g) butter, softened
- 4 ¹/₂ oz (125 g) superfine sugar
- 2 large eggs
- 2–3 tablespoons whole milk

For the topping:
- 1 egg white
- 4 oz (100 g) confectioners' sugar
- food coloring
- candies, to decorate

1 Preheat the oven to 350°F / 180°C.

2 Sift the flour into a bowl, followed by the butter. Use the tips of your fingers to rub the butter and flour together until the mixture becomes crumbly. Alternatively, ask an adult to use an electric whisk.

3 Add the sugar and mix it in, then stir in the eggs. Finally, add the milk to make the mixture creamy.

4 Put spoonfuls of the mixture into the cupcake cases. Bake the cupcakes for 10–15 minutes, until they are golden brown, then leave them to cool on a rack.

5 To make the topping, beat the egg white in a small bowl. Sift the confectioners' sugar into the bowl and beat the mixture until the frosting becomes smooth and thick.

6 Spoon two thirds of the frosting onto each cupcake, smoothing down with a knife or spatula. Leave the frosting to set and then repeat the process, this time adding food coloring to the remaining frosting and using a frosting syringe to add the finer pirate details.

7 Top with candies to finish.

TOP TIP!
Why not give each of your pirates a different face?

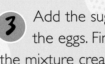

EASTER CUPCAKES

Ingredients:

- 4 1/2 oz (125 g) all-purpose flour with raising agents
- 4 1/2 oz (125 g) butter, softened
- 4 1/2 oz (125 g) superfine sugar
- 2 large eggs
- 2–3 tablespoons whole milk

For the topping:

- a few drops of vanilla extract
- 4 oz (100 g) whipped cream
- mini chocolate eggs
- candy sprinkles

1 Preheat the oven to 350°F / 180°C.

2 Sift the flour into a bowl, followed by the butter. Use the tips of your fingers to rub the butter and flour together until the mixture becomes crumbly. Alternatively, ask an adult to use an electric whisk.

3 Add the sugar and mix it in, then stir in the eggs. Finally, add the milk to make the mixture creamy.

4 Put spoonfuls of the mixture into the cupcake cases. Bake the cupcakes for 10–15 minutes, until they are golden brown, then leave them to cool on a rack.

5 For the topping, add the vanilla extract to the whipped cream and then swirl over each of the cupcakes.

6 Top each with a mini chocolate egg and candy sprinkles.

TOP TIP! Change the topping to reflect the season for a year-round treat!

MINI CUPCAKES

Extra equipment:
- mini cupcake pan
- mini cupcake cases
- piping bag

Ingredients:
- 4 1/2 oz (125 g) all-purpose flour with raising agents
- 4 1/2 oz (125 g) butter, softened
- 4 1/2 oz (125 g) superfine sugar
- 2 large eggs
- 2–3 tablespoons whole milk

For the topping:
- 5 oz (140 g) butter, softened
- 10 oz (280 g) confectioners' sugar
- 1–2 tablespoons whole milk
- edible flowers, to decorate

1 Preheat the oven to 350°F / 180°C.

2 Sift the flour into a bowl, followed by the butter. Use the tips of your fingers to rub the butter and flour together until the mixture becomes crumbly. Alternatively, ask an adult to use an electric whisk.

3 Add the sugar and mix it in, then stir in the eggs.

4 Finally, add the milk to make the mixture creamy.

5 Put spoonfuls of the mixture into the mini cupcake cases. Bake the cupcakes for 8–10 minutes, until they are golden brown, then leave them to cool on a rack.

6 For the topping, place the butter in a large bowl and add half of the confectioners' sugar. Beat until smooth. Add the remaining confectioners' sugar and one tablespoon of the milk and beat the mixture until creamy and smooth. Beat in more milk if necessary to loosen the frosting.

7 Place the topping into a piping bag and pipe over each of the mini cupcakes.

8 Finish with an edible flower and serve.

TOP TIP! Always allow your cupcakes to completely cool before decorating.

47

BIRTHDAY CUPCAKES

Extra equipment:
• candles

Ingredients:
• 4 ¹/₂ oz (125 g) all-purpose flour with raising agents
• 4 ¹/₂ oz (125 g) butter, softened
• 4 ¹/₂ oz (125 g) superfine sugar
• 2 large eggs
• 2–3 tablespoons whole milk

For the topping:
• a few drops of vanilla extract
• whipped cream
• candy sprinkles
• candles, to decorate

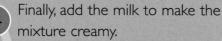

1 Preheat the oven to 350°F / 180°C.

2 Sift the flour into a bowl, followed by the butter. Use the tips of your fingers to rub the butter and flour together until the mixture becomes crumbly. Alternatively, ask an adult to use an electric whisk.

3 Add the sugar and mix it in, then stir in the eggs.

4 Finally, add the milk to make the mixture creamy.

5 Put spoonfuls of the mixture into the cupcake cases. Bake the cupcakes for 10–15 minutes, until they are golden brown, then leave them to cool on a rack.

6 For the topping, add the vanilla extract to the whipped cream and then swirl over each of the cupcakes.

7 Then, top each with candy sprinkles and a candle.

TOP TIP!
Try color coordinating your candy sprinkles with your candles and cases!

CANDY CUPCAKES

Extra equipment:
- piping bag

Ingredients:
- 4 ½ oz (125 g) all-purpose flour with raising agents
- 4 ½ oz (125 g) butter, softened
- 4 ½ oz (125 g) superfine sugar
- 2 large eggs
- 2–3 tablespoons whole milk
- candies

For the topping:
- 5 oz (140 g) butter, softened
- 10 oz (280 g) confectioners' sugar
- 1–2 tablespoons whole milk
- candies of your choice, to decorate

1 Preheat the oven to 350°F / 180°C.

2 Sift the flour into a bowl, followed by the butter. Use the tips of your fingers to rub the butter and flour together until the mixture becomes crumbly. Alternatively, ask an adult to use an electric whisk.

3 Add the sugar and mix it in, then stir in the eggs. Finally, add the milk to make the mixture creamy.

4 Put spoonfuls of the mixture into the cupcake cases, filling them halfway. Drop a few candies on top of the mixture and then top with the remaining mixture.

5 Bake the cupcakes for 15–18 minutes, until they are golden brown, then leave them to cool on a rack.

6 For the topping, place the butter in a large bowl and add half of the confectioners' sugar. Beat until smooth. Add the remaining confectioners' sugar and one tablespoon of the milk and beat the mixture until creamy and smooth. Beat in more milk if necessary to loosen the frosting.

7 Place the topping in a piping bag and pipe onto the top of each cupcake. Finish with a selection of candies.

TOP TIP! Experiment with different-shaped nozzles to achieve varied topping looks!

RASPBERRY & WHITE CHOCOLATE CUPCAKES

TOP TIP!
If you can't find any fresh raspberries, buy frozen ones. Just let them defrost before using them for your cupcakes.

MAKES 12

Extra equipment:
- piping bag

Ingredients:
- 4 ½ oz (125 g) all-purpose flour with raising agents
- 4 ½ oz (125 g) butter, softened
- 4 ½ oz (125 g) superfine sugar
- 2 large eggs
- 2–3 tablespoons whole milk
- 24 raspberries

For the topping:
- 4 oz (100 g) white chocolate
- 5 oz (150 g) butter
- 5 oz (150 g) confectioners' sugar
- 12 raspberries, to decorate
- milk chocolate, grated

1 Preheat the oven to 350°F / 180°C.

2 Sift the flour into a bowl, followed by the butter. Use the tips of your fingers to rub the butter and flour together until the mixture becomes crumbly. Alternatively, ask an adult to use an electric whisk.

3 Add the sugar and mix it in, then stir in the eggs.

4 Finally, add the milk to make the mixture creamy.

5 Put spoonfuls of the mixture into the cupcake cases, filling them halfway. Drop two raspberries on top of the mixture and then top with the remaining mixture.

6 Bake the cupcakes for 15–18 minutes, until they are golden brown, then leave them to cool on a rack.

7 For the topping, ask an adult to melt the white chocolate, either in a microwave or in a pan. Leave to cool.

8 Next, sift the confectioners' sugar into a bowl, add the butter and beat together. Then add the white chocolate and mix until smooth. Place in a piping bag and pipe onto the top of each cupcake.

9 Finish with a raspberry and add twists of grated milk chocolate.

50

PRINCESS CUPCAKES

Extra equipment:
• candles

Ingredients:
• 4 oz (100 g) all-purpose flour with raising agents
• 1 tablespoon cocoa powder
• 4 1/2 oz (125 g) butter, softened
• 4 1/2 oz (125 g) superfine sugar
• 2 large eggs
• 2–3 tablespoons whole milk

For the topping:
• a few drops of vanilla extract
• 4 oz (100 g) whipped cream
• candy sprinkles
• candles, to decorate

1 Preheat the oven to 350°F / 180°C.

2 Sift the flour and cocoa powder into a bowl.

3 Put the butter in the bowl. Use the tips of your fingers to rub the butter, flour and cocoa powder together until the mixture becomes crumbly. Alternatively, ask an adult to use an electric whisk.

4 Add the sugar and mix it in, then stir in the eggs.

5 Finally, add the milk to make the mixture creamy.

6 Put spoonfuls of the mixture into the cupcake cases. Bake the cupcakes for 10–15 minutes, then leave them to cool on a rack.

7 For the topping, add the vanilla extract to the whipped cream. Place in a piping bag, then swirl over each of the cupcakes.

8 Top each with candy sprinkles and girlie candles.

TOP TIP!
Set a timer so you don't forget about your cupcakes cooking in the oven!

SOCCER CUPCAKES

MAKES 12

TOP TIP!
Before decorating your cupcakes, brush the tops lightly with your finger to remove any crumbs.

Extra equipment:
- piping bag with a thin nozzle
- rolling pin
- frosting syringe

Ingredients:
- 4 ¹/₂ oz (125 g) all-purpose flour with raising agents
- 4 ¹/₂ oz (125 g) butter, softened
- 4 ¹/₂ oz (125 g) superfine sugar
- 2 large eggs
- 2–3 tablespoons whole milk

For the topping:
- 5 oz (140 g) butter, softened
- 10 oz (280 g) confectioners' sugar
- 1–2 tablespoons whole milk
- green food coloring
- red food coloring
- ready-to-use frosting

1. Preheat the oven to 350°F / 180°C.

2. Sift the flour into a bowl, followed by the butter. Use the tips of your fingers to rub the butter and flour together until the mixture becomes crumbly. Add the sugar and mix it in, then stir in the eggs. Finally, add the milk to make the mixture creamy.

3. Put spoonfuls of the mixture into the cupcake cases. Bake the cupcakes for 10–15 minutes, until they are golden brown, then leave them to cool on a rack.

4. For the topping, place the butter in a large bowl and add half of the confectioners' sugar. Beat until smooth. Add the remaining confectioners' sugar and one tablespoon of the milk and beat the mixture until creamy and smooth. Beat in more milk if necessary to loosen the frosting. Reserve a quarter of the frosting for later and then add a few drops of green food coloring and mix well.

5. Place the mixture into a piping bag with a thin nozzle. Next, pipe the topping onto the cupcakes, swirling and lifting the nozzle upwards to create a grass-like effect.

6. Next, knead red food coloring into the ready-to-use frosting. Roll it out and ask an adult to cut out shirt shapes, using a sharp knife. Place a shirt onto each of the cupcakes. Using a frosting syringe, pipe a number onto the top of each shirt with the reserved frosting from earlier.

LAVENDER CUPCAKES

Extra equipment:
- blender

Ingredients:
- 1/4 teaspoon dried lavender flowers
- 4 1/2 oz (125 g) superfine sugar
- 4 1/2 oz (125 g) butter, softened
- 2 large eggs
- 4 1/2 oz (125 g) all-purpose flour with raising agents
- 2–3 tablespoons whole milk

For the topping:
- 5 oz (140 g) butter, softened
- 10 oz (280 g) confectioners' sugar
- 1–2 tablespoons whole milk
- candies, to decorate

1 Preheat the oven to 350°F / 180°C.

2 Place the lavender flowers into a blender and ask an adult to process.

3 Add the flowers to a bowl, followed by the sugar and butter. Mix well to combine and then beat in the eggs.

4 Sift in the flour and fold to combine. Finally, add the milk to make the mixture creamy.

5 Put spoonfuls of the mixture into the cupcake cases. Bake the cupcakes for 10–15 minutes, until they are golden brown, then leave them to cool on a rack.

6 For the topping, place the butter in a large bowl and add half of the confectioners' sugar. Beat until smooth. Add the remaining confectioners' sugar and one tablespoon of the milk and beat the mixture until creamy and smooth. Beat in more milk if necessary to loosen the frosting.

7 Swirl the topping onto the cupcakes and top with candies of your choice.

TOP TIP!
Use a fork to eat some of the creamier cupcakes! You don't want to make a mess!

LEMON MERINGUE CUPCAKES

TOP TIP! If you have any left over meringue, crumble it in a bowl and top with fresh berries and cream!

MAKES 12

Extra equipment:
- blender
- piping bag

Ingredients:
- 4 oz (100 g) superfine sugar
- 4 oz (100 g) butter, softened
- 2 eggs
- zest 2 lemons
- 2–3 tablespoons lemon juice
- 4 oz (100 g) all-purpose flour with raising agents
- 4 tablespoons lemon curd

For the topping:
- 5 oz (140 g) butter, softened
- 10 oz (280 g) confectioners' sugar
- 1–2 tablespoons lemon juice
- a few drops of yellow food coloring
- 1 store-bought meringue
- candy sprinkles

1 Preheat the oven to 350°F / 180°C.

2 Put the sugar and butter in a bowl and beat well together. Add the eggs, one by one, mixing in well each time.

3 Stir in the zest and a squeeze of lemon juice, then fold in the flour. If the mixture is a bit stiff, add more lemon juice.

4 Put spoonfuls of the mixture into the cupcake cases, filling them halfway. Add 1 teaspoon of lemon curd and then top with the remaining mixture. Bake the cupcakes for 10–15 minutes, until they are golden brown, then leave them to cool on a rack.

5 For the topping, place the butter in a large bowl and add half of the confectioners' sugar. Beat until smooth.

6 Add the remaining confectioners' sugar, one tablespoon of the lemon juice, and a few drops of yellow food coloring. Beat the mixture until creamy and smooth. Beat in more lemon juice if necessary to loosen the frosting.

7 Then, break up the meringue into tiny pieces. Add to the topping mixture and mix in thoroughly.

8 Place in a piping bag and pipe on top of each cupcake. Finish with candy sprinkles.

54

CHOCOLATE MESS CUPCAKES

Ingredients:

- 4 oz (100 g) all-purpose flour with raising agents
- 1 tablespoon cocoa powder
- 4 1/2 oz (125 g) butter, softened
- 4 1/2 oz (125 g) superfine sugar
- 2 large eggs
- 2–3 tablespoons whole milk
- 2 oz (50 g) chocolate chips

For the topping:

- 7 oz (200 g) bittersweet chocolate
- 1 oz (25 g) butter
- 2 tablespoons heavy cream
- milk chocolate, grated

1 Preheat the oven to 350°F / 180°C.

2 Sift the flour and cocoa powder into a bowl.

3 Put the butter in the bowl. Use the tips of your fingers to rub the butter, flour and cocoa powder together until the mixture becomes crumbly. Alternatively, ask an adult to use an electric whisk.

4 Add the sugar and mix it in, then stir in the eggs.

5 Finally, add the milk to make the mixture creamy, followed by the chocolate chips.

6 Put spoonfuls of the mixture into the cupcake cases. Bake the cupcakes for 10–15 minutes, then leave them to cool on a rack.

7 For the topping, ask an adult to help you put some water in a saucepan over a medium heat. Put the chocolate, butter and cream in a heatproof bowl on top, making sure the bowl doesn't touch the water. Melt the ingredients, stirring the mixture with a wooden spoon.

8 Spoon the melted chocolate on top of each cupcake and leave to set. Once cool, top with grated milk chocolate.

TOP TIP!
Don't worry if these cupcakes look messy—that's what they're all about!

ZINGY LIME CUPCAKES

Extra equipment:
- piping bag

Ingredients:
- 4 ½ oz (125 g) all-purpose flour with raising agents
- 4 ½ oz (125 g) butter, softened
- 4 ½ oz (125 g) superfine sugar
- 2 large eggs
- 2–3 tablespoons whole milk
- 2 teaspoons grated lime zest

For the topping:
- ½ teaspoon lime zest
- ½ teaspoon vanilla extract
- a few drops of green food coloring
- 4 oz (100 g) whipped cream
- candy sprinkles

1 Preheat the oven to 350°F / 180°C.

2 Sift the flour into a bowl, followed by the butter. Use the tips of your fingers to rub the butter and flour together until the mixture becomes crumbly. Alternatively, ask an adult to use an electric whisk.

3 Add the sugar and mix it in, then stir in the eggs.

4 Add the milk to make the mixture creamy, followed by the lime zest.

5 Put spoonfuls of the mixture into the cupcake cases. Bake the cupcakes for 10–15 minutes, until they are golden brown, then leave them to cool on a rack.

6 For the topping, add the lime zest, vanilla extract and a few drops of green food coloring to the whipped cream, beating until smooth.

7 Place in a piping bag and pipe onto the top of each cupcake. Finish with candy sprinkles.

TOP TIP!
One lime should give you enough zest for the entire batch.

CHEEKY CHERRY CUPCAKES

Extra equipment:
- blender
- piping bag

Ingredients:
- 4 ½ oz (125 g) butter, softened
- 4 oz (100 g) bittersweet chocolate, broken into pieces
- 10 ½ oz (300 g) morello cherry jelly
- 5 oz (150 g) superfine sugar
- 2 large eggs, beaten
- 5 oz (150 g) all-purpose flour with raising agents

For the topping:
- 4 oz (100 g) cherries, chopped
- 5 oz (140 g) butter, softened
- 10 oz (280 g) confectioners' sugar
- 2 drops red food coloring
- a few drops of vanilla extract
- 6 teaspoons cherry juice
- 12 fresh or glacé cherries, to decorate

1 Preheat the oven to 350°F / 180°C.

2 Put the butter in a pan and ask an adult to melt it on a medium heat. When nearly melted, stir in the chocolate. Take off the heat and stir until the mixture is smooth and melted.

3 Now, add the cherry jelly, sugar, and eggs. Stir well to combine.

4 Next, sift in the all-purpose flour with raising agents, and mix well.

5 Put spoonfuls of the mixture into the cupcake cases. Bake the cupcakes for 10–15 minutes, then leave them to cool on a rack.

6 For the topping, place the chopped cherries in a blender and ask an adult to process until smooth. Once smooth, add to a bowl, along with the butter, vanilla extract and juice. Then, sift in the confectioners' sugar, add the red food coloring and mix well.

7 Place the topping into a piping bag and pipe onto each cupcake. Finish with a fresh or glacé cherry.

TOP TIP!
You can use fresh or glacé cherries for this cheeky recipe!

FUNNY FACE CUPCAKES

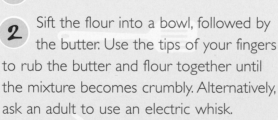

TOP TIP!
You can buy plastic features from hobby stores or toy shops. Also, keep an eye out for funny cases!

MAKES 12

Extra equipment:
- piping bag with a thin nozzle

Ingredients:
- 4 1/2 oz (125 g) all-purpose flour with raising agents
- 4 1/2 oz (125 g) butter, softened
- 4 1/2 oz (125 g) superfine sugar
- 2 large eggs
- 2–3 tablespoons whole milk

For the topping:
- 5 oz (140 g) butter, softened
- 10 oz (280 g) confectioners' sugar
- 1–2 tablespoons whole milk
- a few drops of food coloring x 3 different colors
- store-bought decorations or candies

1 Preheat the oven to 350°F / 180°C.

2 Sift the flour into a bowl, followed by the butter. Use the tips of your fingers to rub the butter and flour together until the mixture becomes crumbly. Alternatively, ask an adult to use an electric whisk.

3 Add the sugar and mix it in, then stir in the eggs.

4 Finally, add the milk to make the mixture creamy.

5 Put spoonfuls of the mixture into the cupcake cases. Bake the cupcakes for 10–15 minutes, until they are golden brown, then leave them to cool on a rack.

6 For the topping, place the butter in a large bowl and add half of the confectioners' sugar. Beat until smooth. Add the remaining confectioners' sugar and one tablespoon of the milk and beat the mixture until creamy and smooth. Beat in more milk if necessary to loosen the frosting. Next, divide up the topping into three portions and add different food colorings to each.

7 Place the first color into a piping bag and pipe the topping onto four of the cupcakes. Repeat the topping process, this time with the different colors.

8 Finish the faces with funny features. Use store-bought decorations or candies to create the funniest faces you can think of!

CHOCOLATE & PEANUT BUTTER CUPCAKES

Extra equipment:
- piping bag

Ingredients:
- 8 oz (225 g) light brown sugar
- 2 oz (50 g) butter, softened
- 4 1/2 oz (125 g) chocolate spread
- 2 eggs
- a few drops of vanilla extract
- 5 oz (150 g) all-purpose flour
- 3 oz (75 g) cocoa powder
- 2 teaspoons baking powder
- 3 fl.oz (100 ml) whole milk

For the topping:
- 4 tablespoons butter, softened
- 8 oz (225 g) cream cheese
- 6 oz (170 g) smooth peanut butter
- 12 oz (350 g) confectioners' sugar
- 4 oz (100 g) whipped cream

1 Preheat the oven to 350°F / 180°C.

2 Beat the light brown sugar and butter together until smooth and then add the chocolate spread and mix together thoroughly.

3 Add the eggs, one at a time, beating well after each addition, and then add the vanilla extract.

4 Sift the flour, cocoa powder and baking powder together and fold into the mixture, along with the milk.

5 Put spoonfuls of the mixture into the cupcake cases.

6 Bake the cupcakes for 20–25 minutes, then leave them to cool on a rack.

7 For the topping, beat the butter, cream cheese, and smooth peanut butter until blended.

8 Add the confectioners' sugar slowly, then add the whipped cream and beat until smooth and creamy.

9 Place the topping into a piping bag and swirl onto each of the cupcakes.

TOP TIP! Sprinkle peanuts on top for a double nut hit!

DAISY CUPCAKES

TOP TIP!
Experiment with different petal shapes. Try to make your favorite flower!

MAKES 12–15

Extra equipment:
• rolling pin

Ingredients:
• 5 oz (150 g) all-purpose flour with raising agents
• 2 tablespoons cocoa powder
• 5 oz (150 g) butter, softened
• 5 oz (150 g) superfine sugar
• 3 eggs
• a few drops of vanilla extract
• 1–2 tablespoons whole milk

To decorate:
• ready-to-use frosting
• food coloring
• candies

1 Preheat the oven to 350°F / 180°C.

2 Sift the flour and cocoa powder into a bowl. Add the butter and use the tips of your fingers to rub the butter, flour and cocoa powder together until the mixture becomes crumbly.

3 Add the sugar and mix it in. Now stir in the eggs. Finally, add a few drops of vanilla extract and the milk to make the mixture creamy. Stir well.

4 Put spoonfuls of the mixture into the cupcake cases. Bake the cakes for 10–15 minutes, then leave them to cool on a rack.

5 To decorate the cupcakes with frosting, knead a few drops of food coloring into half of the ready-to-use frosting and roll it out until the color is evenly spaced.

6 Ask an adult to cut the frosting into flower shapes, then place on each cake.

7 Next, do the same to the other half of the frosting, this time with a different color. Ask an adult to cut out smaller petal shapes using a sharp knife. Run a knife along the top of each petal, before placing them over the first layer of frosting, gently pressing down.

8 Top with a candy to finish.

CARAMEL CUPCAKES

Ingredients:

- 4 oz (100 g) bittersweet chocolate
- 5 oz (150 g) butter
- 5 oz (150 g) brown sugar
- 3 oz (75 g) light corn syrup
- 5 fl.oz (150 ml) whole milk
- 4 ½ oz (125 g) all-purpose flour
- 2 oz (50 g) all-purpose flour with raising agents
- 1 egg, lightly beaten

For the topping:

- 1 oz (25 g) butter, softened
- 2 oz (50 g) soft brown sugar
- 2 tablespoons light cream
- 4 oz (100 g) confectioners' sugar
- chocolate, to decorate
- fudge, to decorate

1 Preheat the oven to 350°F / 180°C.

2 Place the chocolate, butter, brown sugar, syrup and milk in a small saucepan. Ask an adult to stir over a low heat until melted and smooth. Leave to cool for about 15 minutes.

3 Sift the all-purpose flour and all-purpose flour with raising agents into a bowl.

4 Then add the flour into the caramel mixture. Next, stir in the egg. Mix until combined.

5 Use a teaspoon to transfer equal amounts of the mixture into the cupcake cases. Bake the cupcakes for about 20 minutes. Leave them to cool on a rack.

6 For the topping, ask an adult to melt the butter and sugar in a saucepan. Bring to the boil, add the cream and simmer for 5 minutes. Remove from the heat and sift in the confectioners' sugar. Beat until smooth.

7 Swirl over the cupcakes and top with smaller pieces of chocolate and fudge.

TOP TIP!
Experiment with the decorations! Why not try candy sprinkles or chopped chocolate bars for the topping?

CHOCOLATE FUDGE CUPCAKES

Ingredients:

- 2 oz (50 g) superfine sugar
- 2 oz (50 g) soft brown sugar
- 4 oz (100 g) butter, softened
- 2 eggs
- 2 tablespoons condensed milk
- 4 ½ oz (125 g) all-purpose flour with raising agents
- 1 teaspoon baking powder
- 1 oz (25 g) unsweetened cocoa powder

For the topping:

- 5 oz (150 g) butter
- 5 oz (150 g) sifted confectioners' sugar
- 4 tablespoons cocoa powder
- 3 tablespoons whole milk
- candy sprinkles, to decorate

1 Preheat the oven to 350°F / 180°C.

2 Place both sugars and the butter into a bowl and beat together until smooth.

3 Then, add the eggs, one at a time, and mix well.

4 Add the condensed milk and then sift in the flour, baking powder and cocoa powder, making sure they are well mixed.

5 Put spoonfuls of the mixture into the cupcake cases. Bake the cupcakes for 20–25 minutes, then leave them to cool on a rack.

6 For the topping, place the butter in a large bowl and add half of the confectioners' sugar. Beat until smooth.

7 Add the remaining confectioners' sugar, cocoa powder and one tablespoon of the milk and beat the mixture until creamy and smooth. Beat in more milk if necessary to loosen the frosting.

8 Swirl the topping onto each of the cupcakes and finish with candy sprinkles.

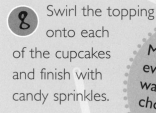

TOP TIP!
Make this cupcake even more mouth-watering by adding chopped pieces of fudge to the topping!

APRICOT CUPCAKES

Extra equipment:
- piping bag

Ingredients:
- 4 oz (100 g) all-purpose flour with raising agents
- 4 ½ oz (125 g) butter, softened
- 4 ½ oz (125 g) superfine sugar
- 2 large eggs
- 4 oz (100 g) ready-to-eat apricots, chopped
- 2–3 tablespoons whole milk

For the topping:
- 5 oz (150 g) butter, softened
- 10 oz (280 g) confectioners' sugar
- 1 tablespoon apricot jelly
- 1 drop orange food coloring

1 Preheat the oven to 350°F / 180°C.

2 Sift the flour into a bowl, followed by the butter. Use the tips of your fingers to rub the butter and flour together until the mixture becomes crumbly. Alternatively, ask an adult to use an electric whisk.

3 Add the sugar and mix it in, then stir in the eggs.

4 Finally, add the chopped apricots and milk to make the mixture creamy.

5 Put spoonfuls of the mixture into the cupcake cases. Bake the cupcakes for 10–15 minutes, until they are golden brown, then leave them to cool on a rack.

6 For the topping, place the butter in a large bowl and add half of the confectioners' sugar. Beat until smooth.

7 Add the remaining confectioners' sugar, and one tablespoon of apricot jelly and the food coloring and beat the mixture until creamy and smooth. Beat in some milk if necessary to loosen the frosting.

8 Place into a piping bag and pipe the topping onto the cupcakes.

TOP TIP!
You can use either dried or fresh apricots depending on availability.

63

INDEX OF RECIPES

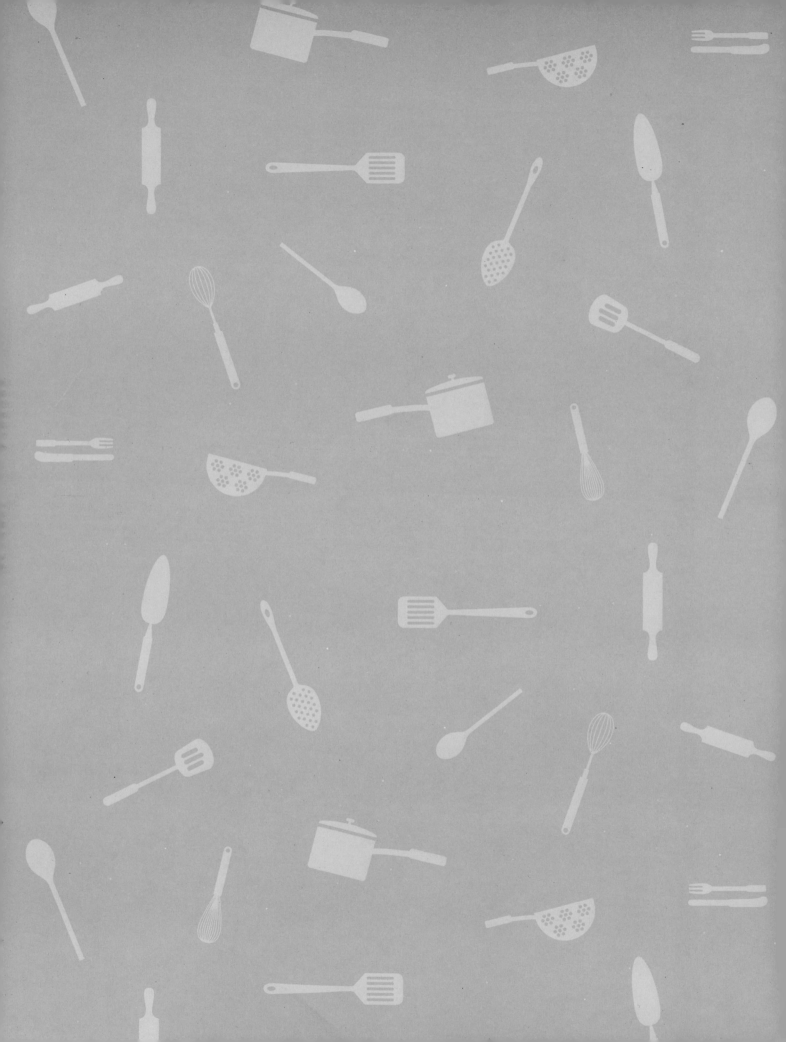